Countryside And Coastal Notes
A Poetry Notebook

Suzanne McDonough

Dedication

To Geoff – For introducing me to wonderful
Northumberland all those years ago.

Acknowledgements

To the editors of the following publications in which some of these poems first appeared: Reach Poetry – A Poetry Society Landmark magazine, All Our Days Anthology, Special Places Anthology.

Contents

Countryside And Coastal Notes

Northumberland's unmistakable landscape is a combination of moorland and pasture, field and forest, each part cleverly divided by a complicated network of man-made restrictions.

One such restriction is the hedgerow, home to wildlife in the summer providing birds with a nest site, and in later months it can be a provider of both food and shelter.

But often the more visible are the dry stone walls weaving across the land, stretching wide across the open countryside. The walls keep the livestock from straying, and also provide shelter from the harsh winds and bleak winter weather.

Walking through the countryside or next to the coast can be both stimulating and rewarding, take a good look around and note what you see.

A hazy warm sunny day, in the distance the lighthouse surrounded by a thin blanket of sea fret. This will roll in and roll out depending on the tide.

Bees on lavender and dense clover protecting the ground; a blanket of buttercups the most familiar of summer flowers covering pastures everywhere. Giant hogweed lining the pathway, a robust bristly plant with coarse foliage and flat top white flower heads. And the dandelion used as flavouring for wine food for pets or a salad vegetable, a complex recognisable weed.

Closer to the coast and the cliff edge, brambles appear with delicate white flowers. Ground elder shows its umbrella shaped head above the common nettle, which attracts many different butterflies.

A striking plant of coastal dunes and shingle banks, with its large yellow flowers and blue-green foliage is the yellow horned poppy. The dainty little burnet rose is also most common near to the sea. It spreads by its suckers to cover a large area, and its creamy white flowers stand out against its many leaves.

Seabirds come ashore to nest during the late spring and summer. Cliffs attract kittiwakes and cormorants, and behind sandy and shingle beaches nest gulls, ringed plovers, and oystercatchers.

A kestrel hovers above neighbouring woodland, and along the winding track burrows appear offering shelter and concealment for rabbits and foxes. This area of wetland offers protection to ducks and geese, including the eider which nests near to the coast. It lines its nest with soft breast feathers known as eider down, and lives in offshore waters. A yellow flag iris boldly sways in the breeze, along with the sweet scented honeysuckle. Night flying moths are attracted by the scent, which is strongest at dusk, and pollinate the flowers as they seek nectar. The honeysuckle is a favourite hedgerow plant.

The tide is now coming in, and the waves gently embrace the beach. The air is filled with the scent of countryside flowers, and the sea.

So next time you are out and about, remember countryside or coast hedgerows or sea, there is no better place to be. Whatever the season. Enjoy.•

A Coastal Retreat

The day was dark and uneventful.
The weather had deteriorated,
And torrential rain fell from heavy black clouds.
Sleet tapped on the window
And swirled around the garden
A thin white blanket covered the ground
Crocuses were lost in the gentle snow
As daffodils greeted the land graciously
In the roaring noise of the wind.

The outlook changed day by day
But the lighthouse remained the same.
The sky was reflected in the sea
A gloomy grey and a brilliant blue,
And, this was the view
From a small wooden window overlooking the sea.

According To Joseph – For Joe and Sam

When you are 3
What do you see
When looking at the coast?
White fluffy clouds
Waves crashing on rocks
Or, just maybe lots of water.

When you are 3
What do you see
When looking at the lighthouse?
White washed walls
White light shining bright
Or, just maybe a house for dragons.

When you are 3
What do you see
When looking at Uncle Geoff's house?
Wonderful structure
Wow, look at the view
Or, just maybe a place to get pizza.

Such innocence is a joy to behold long may it last!

Actually

Actually, is a funny word
In a strange kind of way,
What does it mean?
What does it say?

I love and miss you deeply
Whenever you're away,
Actually, I do.
So what does it say?

It exists as fact
Not imagined
And tells us strongly so,
Not estimated or guessed,
A real word
Surprisingly,
So.

Autumn

The season of the year
Between summer and winter
When leaves change colour and fall,
Leaving bare branches broken and twisted
Leaving trees barren and tall.

Jewelled tones cover the ground
A rich blanket of copper and brown
Amber and bronze leaves scatter
As little feet patter,
Through the dense woodland floor.

Catching the cool autumn light
The lovely broad-leaved helleborine
Is a truly magnificent sight
And, a tall rather uncommon orchid
Usually found deep in the shade
Bends slowly accepting the changes
Of the seasons about to be made.

Do I Follow The Flow?

I need some focus in my life
Which way do I go?
Is it time for a change
Maybe,
Or do I follow the flow?

The pros and cons are all weighed up
But I still can't decide,
Do I follow the flow?
Or wait for a change in the tide

The tide comes in
The tide goes out
Day and Night's the same,
Do I follow the flow?
Or play it as a game

Only one person can decide
I know my friend it's true,
Whichever path you take
Always be true to you.

Inseparable

Walking the narrow cobbled streets
With white washed walls
I feel the warm stone
And my fingers caress history and all it holds.
The ornate doorways share special secrets
Of times gone by
A treasure trove full of wonder and discovery
Magic and myths,
Memories and dreams.
I feel the warm air on my face
And sigh with relief,
Pleased I have made the journey
And returned to our perfect place
My heart is captured once again
And so the love affair begins
I look at you and smile.

Iris

Purple shadows in the night
Silhouetted against the light
Fragrant scent fills the air
Delicate petals leaves so green
The prettiest flowers I have ever seen.

Contrasting colours vivid and bright
Purple, lilac, blue and white.

A dash of yellow joins them all
My lovely Iris stands so tall!

For Jack

I remember Jack
His pointed face, eyes wide and brown
A funny shaped ear hiding a frown
He walked with a limp an old injury
But it didn't stop him chasing birds out of trees.
He loved the chase
And winning the race
Battling to the end
He was my dearest greyhound friend.

Lets go racing
He would run
As if the race had been won
Faster and faster at great speed
He would always take the lead.
Now have a rest
Don't get too tired
It's time for sleep
And in the early hours
As darkness falls
Shadows call
Keep on running to the end
Sweet dreams my dearest greyhound friend.

My Soul Mate

I close my eyes
And think of you
And all our time together,
I know I have found my soul mate
A best friend to love forever

No matter where we go
We are together as one
Over land or sea
Miles apart
We were always meant to be,
My love.
My chosen one!

Lead Me To The Shore

Gazing over the fields and fences
Heading for the trees,
Looking straight ahead
Hair blowing in the breeze,
Winding tracks,
Sloping tracks,
Many treasures to adore
Violets and seaside pansies
Lead me to the shore.

Footprints left along the way
Only a few people pass,
Could there be wild rabbits hiding in the grass?
The smell of the sea guides me
Just a few paces more,
Violets and seaside pansies
Lead me to the shore.

Life Is So Precious

Life is so precious
Taken for granted most of the time
Make the most of each day,
And you are well on your way
To being happy not sad
Feeling good and not bad.

Life is so precious
And often too short
So, don't hold back
Do what you feel
Open your heart
Where better to start.

Life is so precious
Never look back
Always ahead
Search your soul,
And you are well on your way
To reaching your goal!

Life is so precious
And we all hold the key
To our own wonderful, magical, destiny!

Peace Hope And Love

Footprints left in the fallen snow
People rushing lots of places to go
Brightly wrapped parcels
Held with ribbons and bows,
What's inside?
Nobody knows.

Sparkling baubles
Twinkling lights
Silvery tinsel
What a magical sight.

Snow on the hedgerows
Snow on the ground
Covering rooftops
For miles around
Whatever Christmas means to you,
May *peace hope and love*
Always shine through!

Sea

I can see you
I can hear you
I can smell you
And when the tide is in I can touch you
You are the sea.
The great mass of salt water
Smaller than the ocean
But larger than a lake.

Ridges move across you
Arching and breaking on the shore
The pull of the sun and moon change you
From high to low you rise and fall,
Showing the sea bed
The seaweed
The seashells
I feel the sea breeze
And see change.

Spring

The season between winter and summer
When most plants begin to grow
Wild flowers appear across open meadows
A sea of blue ivy overflows
A charming deep coloured plant
Which creeps between hedgerows and woodland floors
A bitter herb for flavouring ale
Maybe, this is just an old wives tale.

The ivy leads gently down
To a golden beach of yellow marsh marigolds
A most imposing meadow plant
With large golden cup-shaped flowers
It's surrounded by myth and folklore
Holding many secret powers.

Wild daffodils line the pathway
And a few bright bluebells appear
The start of a wonderful springtime
New life, to bring new cheer.

St-Mary's Lighthouse

Tall and white
Shining bright through the night
Keeping boats off jagged rocks
Watching over wayward flocks.
Covered in mist, sea fret, and fog
Watching over wayward seadogs
Standing proud for all to see
Watching over you and me.
Keeping guard while the village sleeps
Watching over those who weep
Disaster strikes lives may be lost
But the lighthouse guides at any cost
Watching over the coast and shoreline
Protecting the region and the Tyne.

St-Mary's Lighthouse is situated on the north east coast at Whitley Bay.
There has been a lighthouse on St-Mary's Island since mediaeval times,
and the present lighthouse was opened in 1898.
It marks the half-distance between Blyth and the Tyne.

Storm Clouds

Silver grey mist hovers
Across the open land,
Pearls of rain dance in the wind
As if hand in hand.

The foghorn sounds
Keeping watch over the open bay,
Many boats will pass the coast
Today on their merry way.

As the sky darkens shadows form
A rumble comes from the sea,
Thunder way in the distance
Lightning flashes in the trees.

The foghorn gets louder and louder
And the thunder roars
Waves crash on the jagged rocks
The rain just pours, and pours.

The rain moves slowly gliding
On to pastures new,
Leaving a vibrant rainbow
May all your dreams come true!

Summer

Between spring and autumn
The warmest season of the year
Extends from May to September
In the northern hemisphere

Lots of wild flowers can be found
Covering meadows and open ground
The meadow cranes-bill with bluish flowers
Strikes out beautifully amongst foxglove towers
A tall majestic purple plant
With generous tubular flowers
Which sway in the breeze to and fro for hours and hours.

A time of greatest energy
When happiness prevails
Good fortune merriment and bliss
Seal this season with a kiss.
Cherish long days and warm evenings spent
Admiring the countryside
With honeysuckle scent.

The Quarry

The light reflects across the water
Shimmering rays of green and blue
Stillness echoes around every tree
Every flower reminds me of you
Wild strawberries, primroses, violets too
All in miniature standing so proud,
What a wonderful place to be,
No longer a face in a crowd.
Alone with my thoughts on a bright sunny day
Autumn will soon be on the way,
The leaves will change colour
From bright green to gold,
What happy thoughts I hold.
Fish dance by the water's edge
And swans glide to the tune
Of whistling wind through the trees,
Of flowers swinging in the breeze,
Leaves rustle under foot
Nature at it s best just take a look.
The pine trees sway as I make my way
To the stile by the end of the gate,
What a wonderful place to be,
Hurry back, Hurry back,
I can't wait.

The Quarry is situated in the Heart of Northumberland. It is a quiet
haven for fishing, walking, and solitary moments of peace.

Warkworth Castle

Boldly, displaying its character to all
Warkworth castle stands so tall,
Looking down on the village
And all within,
Watching with pride as people flood in.

Surrounded by history
And secrets of the past
Following footsteps
Who walked here last? …

In changing seasons you hold your own
A place that's loved and I'm not alone.

The castle and heritage must remain firm
So future generations can look and learn,
And see the daffodils on a spring day
What a wonderful memory to take away!

What A Special Place To Be

The deepest darkest midnight sky
Engulfs the world as time goes by,
The beach is so peaceful
The sea is so still,
The stars shine brightly
In the air there's a chill.

The waves lap gently around our feet
Here together,
Not another soul shall we meet.

Shells glitter in the soft sand
At this moment you take my hand,
Standing close we look out to sea
What a special place to be!

It all looks so different in daylight hours
But nothing can compare
With this secret of ours,
We will look back one day and remember
All the good times we had here
From March to November!

Whitegate

The sky is so blue
The grass is so green
Fields spread before us to pastures unseen.

The countryside is wonderful on a beautiful day
All its qualities appear as we make our way,
Along winding roads, and along leafy lanes,
Reminiscing and sharing our hopes and our aims

Memories flood back of childhood days spent
Walking in hedgerows and smelling the scent,
Of honeysuckle climbing around grandma's door
Her welcoming smile,
For her company once more.

Treasured times of days gone by
It's nice to remember,
As I wipe a tear from my eye.

Winter

The coldest season of the year
Coming between autumn and spring
Wintry winds blow unfriendly and cold
But lots of wild flowers still remain bold
Common field-speedwell can be found
In arable fields and all around
With sky blue flowers and one petal white
Sapphire shades shine so bright

The holly bush thrives in the bleak winter weather
Bearing ruby red berries and glossy green leaves
Home to a robin that sits on the fence post
Providing shelter and cover while a nest does she weave
The sky is dark
And night-time falls
To close the day
Before dawn calls.

Perfection
For Dad

Like a bud you have grown
And shown true character and strength.

Like an open flower you have blossomed
And made your way
Discovered the world
And all within

Like a closed flower you have withdrawn
Quietly to rest
Finding inner peace at last.

A Lonely Figure

Waiting patiently by the window
Looking out over open ground
The outline hovers moving slowly
Disappearing quietly with no sound.
A lost soul searching, for peace and comfort
Roaming the hall with no rest or reprieve
Alone, tormented with grief and tortured
Do spirits ever leave?

(A lonely figure awaits the return of a loved one that never appears)

Reunited

Umbrellas line the beach across the bay
A sea of white domes
Cascade down to the waters edge
People are scattered innocently here and there
Boats sway gently along the waterline
Cool clear turquoise water beacons
Softly rippled by a slight breeze
Another, relaxing day in a place of utter bliss.

Pathways made of rounded stone
Twist and turn
And gradually we learn
To find our way around the village.

Friendly and familiar faces appear
And time passes with such ease
The pace is slow and welcoming
And this is all that we need.
As the sun goes down across the bay
We look forward to a brand new day
Reunited.

Blue Skies

The sound of Lapwings and the sea
Bring me back to reality
And, I cherish all I have today
A special place come what may
.

I have a love for you to see me through
The darkest ever days.

My heart is yours, and yours alone
And, filled with warmth I head for home
Awaiting, your return.

True Love

Romantic Liaisons
Holding hands by moonlight
Under a blanket of stars.

Holding hands by moonlight
Breathing in time to the gentle breeze
And, the sound of breaking waves.

Under a blanket of stars
Hearts entwined
Our love is sealed with a silent kiss
A love to last a life time and beyond
A love that never ends.

Soft White Flakes

Aggressive bursts of snow pass the window
Silently tapping the salt stained pane.

A flurry of shining white beads
Linked by invisible silk disappear into the distance
Hovering over a still March day.

Shining Light

Like a shining light to retrieve
The door is opened
And I breathe - the air of God.

The door is opened
And I am free
To think my own thoughts.

And I breathe - the air of God
Fulfilled at peace at last.

I sit in this magnificent 900-year-old little church and give thanks.

A Place Of Peace

A church built for the Delaval family
On a previous Saxon site
Parts of which can still be found
When exploring the church and its sacred ground.
Brightly coloured stained glass windows
Dating back to Victorian days
Are excellent examples describing the era
Portraying life in different ways.
The windows shine with jewelled colours
And the golden rays of the seasonal sun
Lighting up a place to reflect in silence
When the day is nearly done.

The Church Of Our Lady

In our midst
A splendid thing
A lot of pleasure it does bring
A place of worship and tranquillity
A delightful haven, meant to be.
The Church Of Our Lady is hidden away
To be discovered day after day.

Seaton Delaval Hall

Here stands a magnificent structure built of dark grey cold stone.
A weather beaten monument streaked with purple and brown.
Its towers and columns reach up to the never-ending sky.
This wonderful winter palace is encapsulated by a gnarled oak forest.

Empty eyes watch from large windows high in gigantic walls.

And, the wind howls among the balustraded battlements.

As the sun goes down light forms grey shadows which magically
disappear into the dense woodland.
The watery winter sun sets over open fields
While a crisp wind cuts through the hedgerow.

Singing spirits stir as the north-easterly wind blows.
Laughter echoes across the ploughed land
Sweeping the countryside far and wide
Only to be carried out to sea on an invisible wave.

Changes

Following the closure of Hartley Pitt
Seaton Sluice fell into decline
A seaport no more
Shipping left from different docks
The dock at Blyth
And, the dock at the Tyne.

No coal was shipped from the harbour again
And the bottle works suffered in time
From faraway lands new methods were found
Industrial life had slowed down
And, the past was hidden away
Like miners thoughts in underground shafts
Only to be retrieved another day.

Great community changes were on the way.
Tomorrow is another day,
And, another story.

Notes And Inspirational Thoughts....

Notes And Inspirational Thoughts....

Notes And Inspirational Thoughts....

Notes And Inspirational Thoughts....

On A Final Note....

A Special Thank-You goes to
Susan for all her help and encouragement.

Many Thanks to Roger Harvey for changing
my outlook, and for the guidance he has so
generously shared.

And Thanks to Angie for Write Beside The
Sea, all her support, and may each new day
shower you with new opportunities.

www.ingramcontent.com/pod-product-compliance
Lightning Source LLC
LaVergne TN
LVHW041209080426
835508LV00008B/879